A Dance Across Dimensions

Tales of Nature, Myth, and Imagination

Varane Parsana

BookLeaf Publishing

India | USA | UK

Made with ❤ on the BookLeaf Publishing Platform
www.bookleafpub.in
www.bookleafpub.com

Dedication

"I would like to dedicate these poems to the people who have played an instrumental role in helping me express myself through words. To my teachers, who patiently guided me and taught me the art of creating different types of poetry, your support and encouragement have been invaluable. To my parents, thank you for always encouraging me to write and for suggesting thought-provoking topics that fuel my creativity. And to my elder brother, I am grateful for your thoughtful feedback, which has helped me grow as a poet. This collection is a reflection of your belief in me and the lessons you've all shared."

Preface

"A Dance across Dimensions" explores a diverse variety of themes that reflect the beauty, complexity and wonder of both real and imagined worlds. The poems delve into cultural celebrations like Diwali and Christmas, reflections on mythology, mysteries of space and our cosmic neighbours and importance of the nature around us. With vivid imagery and expressive language, this collection invites readers on a journey through time, space and tradition.

Acknowledgements

1. Spacebound Alien

Alien is in space,
Having a race,
While watching chase.

Alien is in space,
Has red and green face,
With a wobbly brace.

Alien is in space,
Plays with mace,
Has a golden lace.

Alien is in space,
Has a paper to trace,
Doodle at different place.

Alien is in space,
Smiles in embrace,
Finds a new place.

2. Lunarlit Voyage

The moon shines bright, a silvery light,
Reflecting the sun through the night.
In the sky, stars deploy,
Like asteroids, they enjoy,
Guiding us with their glow so bright.

3. The Burden of Measurement

Measurement, measurement, why so tough?
Numbers and units - never enough.
Each calculation, a thread in the sky,
Yet still we wonder, "What?And why?"

Measurement, measurement, why so tough?
From millimeter to kilometer -distance unfolds.
Centimeter to meter, a story is told -
Shortest to longest, never enough.

Measurement, measurement, why so tough?
From gram to kilogram, a gentle rise;
Milligram to metric ton, a vast surprise!
Lightest to heaviest - never enough.

Measurement, measurement, why so tough?
From milliliter to liter, the volume expands.
Centiliter to gallon, the change is grand -
Empty to full, never enough.

Measurement, measurement, why so tough?
Weight and capacity—still not enough.
We measure space, we measure time,
Yet fail to grasp what's truly mine.

4. Under the Christmas Sky

C - Chilled winter night, stars shining bright.

H - Hearts are warm, sharing pure delight.

R - Rudolph the reindeer helping with all his might.

I - In every home love glows so bright.

S - Snowflakes fall soft and white.

T - Together we cherish this holy night.

M - Memorable Moments we make tonight.

A - Amazing Santa gifts all through the night.

S - Season of giving kindness takes flight.

This is the magic of Christmas Night.

5. Inquiring Minds and Robots

Robo Robo, why are you so innovative and Reliable?

Robo Robo, how do you make everything automated and Organized?

Robo Robo, when did you become so famous and Brilliant?

Robo Robo, which code do we use to program and Operate?

Robo Robo, what will you create next with advanced Technology?

6. Avengers Assemble

"Avengers, Avengers helping to stop all dangers
From north to south, east to west".

Hulk is as big as a towering house,
Ant-man shrinks as small as a mouse.
Thor strikes fast like roaring thunder -
A team so strong, they make no blunder.

"Avengers, Avengers helping to stop all dangers
From north to south, east to west".

Captain, the leader, sharp as a jackal,
With courage so fierce, none dare to tackle.
Spidey spins silk, strong as steel,
Swinging through streets with speed and zeal.

"Avengers, Avengers helping to stop all dangers
From north to south, east to west".

7. Shiva- The Cosmic Guardian

Shiva, the Supreme Self, manifested,
Coiled in cosmos with Sheshnag rested.
With a three - pronged spear -so stuck, so strong-
To save spiritual sages from sinister wrong.

The Shivling shines in silver light,
The Serpent Slithers soft and bright.
The saints sing in soulful sound
Seeking blessings where spirits are found.

Shiva stands with Shakti's strength,
The cosmos bends to their divine length.
Son Ganesha with wisdom bright,
Shakti's steadfast guard holds tight.

8. A Sunny Challenge

The sun shines from east to west,
A source of vitamin D, the best.
But when the sun is feeling sad,
It gets a little mad,
And watch out—it's putting you to the test!

9. Journey of Our Cosmic Neighbors

You look up at night,
You can see some light,
Big dots shining bright,
Still wondering what's right.

Mercury, small as well as close,
The Sun is so near, but it doesn't impose,
Days become hot, nights become cold,
Terrestrial planet's dust devils start to fold.

Venus, the hottest and brightest,
Unique rotation makes it the starkest,
Massive lava reshapes the surface,
A planet where fire rules the face.

Earth, the only planet with life,
A world of peace, a world of rife.
Oceans, forests, and mountains so high,
A place where creatures roam and fly.

Mars, the red planet, glowing bright,
No cozy blankets for the night.
Olympus Mons, the biggest volcano,
A giant peak that goes on and on.

"Jupiter's Great Red Spot,
Still spinning like a pot",
Biggest planet in the solar,
A sight we all adore.

"Saturn's orbit full of asteroids,
Made of ice, dust and rocks deployed",
This planet has no atmosphere,
You'll sink if you land, that's clear.

Uranus, spinning on its side,
Having diamonds so wide,
It's so cold out there,
I think it's not fair.

Neptune, the ice giant, distinct and blue,
With 14 moons, a world of hue.
Strangest and wildest weather,
Much larger than Earth, in ways we can't gather.

10. Waterways of God

Ganga flows from heights,
Originated from peaks high,
Shiva's crown below.

Yamuna flows wide,
Born in Himalaya's heart,
Yama's twin beside.

Kaveri smiles in embrace,
From Bramhagiri's hills so high,
Sage Agastya's grace.

Narmada winds through plains,
Created from Mount Riksha,
Daughter of Shiva's perspiration.

Shipra, sacred and clear,
Born from Varah's blessed core,
Vishnu's incarnation, a divine guide.

Godavari, holy flow,
Rises from Ganga's pure stream,
Sage Gautam's blessings glow.

Sarasvati, mighty river,
Goddess of knowledge, music, and art,
In her flow, wisdom finds its place.

11. Dreaming Monster

In the still dark night,
Candles were gleaming bright.

A Monster as big as a house,
Ears as tiny as a mouse.

Eyes as sharp as an eagle's gaze,
Feet as webbed as a seagull's ways.

Fangs as long as a sharpened spear,
The monster is drawing near.

Hands as huge as a giant's face,
Legs as thin as a spider's trace.

I held my breath, too scared to scream,
I woke up, it was just a dream.

12. Vantara - Where Dreams and Nature Meet

In Jamnagar's heart, where the wild winds blow,
Vantara World stands, where injured animals grow.
Three thousand acres, a sanctuary wide,
Where healing and hope in silence reside.

Van—a forest, vast and grand,
Tara—the stars that light the land.
Two thousand souls of forty-three kinds,
Each with a story, each with their minds.

With gentle hands and hearts full of care,
They heal the wounds from habitat loss and despair.
In the face of poaching, both wild and captive,
They give the creatures hope, strong and active.

A Mamba from Africa, swift and bold,
Now finds solace, away from the cold.
A Kangaroo from Australia, full of grace,
Leaps with joy in a safer space.

A Spix's Macaw from Brazil's bright skies,
Sings once more, with gleaming eyes.
A one-horned Rhino from Asia's plains,
Now heals in peace, away from chains.

An Inland Taipan from Australia's land,
Endangered and rare, in Vantara's hand.
A Fennec Fox from the Saharan heat,
With ears so large, so nimble on its feet.

Inauguration by Narendra Modi,
A moment of change, a future to see.
A place of hope, where young hearts will grow,
In the embrace of nature, love will flow.

Waiting to see the sanctuary unfold,
A vision of peace, a story to be told.
A haven of dreams, where children can play,
Learning from nature in a special way.

13. Cricket Carnival

IPL - The Festival of Cricket
Ignites the cricketing flame,
Where every player rises to fame.

SRH - The Power Within
Head hits the ball with a mighty swing,
The stadium roars as the ball takes wing.

RCB - The Spin of Glory
Bethel spins the ball so cool,
Leaving batsmen trapped like a fool.

CSK - The Steady Power
Ravindra always ready,
In a position that makes him steady.

GT - The Elegance of Gill
Gill hits the ball lightly,
As he holds the bat tightly.

MI - The Power of Pandya
Pandya rounds well, with strength and grace,
Charging forward, setting the pace.

LSG - The All-Round Brilliance
Marsh, with bat and ball, does it all,
His every move, a masterful call.

RR - The Explosive Jaiswal
Jaiswal's bat crackles with fire,
Each shot he plays takes the team higher.

DC - The Lightning of Starc
Starc bowls with fury, pace, and might,
Batsmen tremble with fright as he takes flight.

PBKS - The Versatile Jansen
Jansen's skill, both bat and ball,
A true all-rounder, answering the call.

KKR - The Dazzling Singh
Singh's bat strikes with explosive power,
Every hit, a thrilling moment to tower.

IPL - The Global Unity
Players from the world, together they stand,
One united community, no boundary in land.

14. Diwali Radiance

Diwali oh Diwali
Making people buy crackling sparks tonight,
Rockets and twine bombs go boomy and bright,
Flower pots and spinners bring colors to sight,
A dazzling dance of fire, a radiant light.

Diwali oh Diwali
Making people crave the sweetest treats,
Chocolates, laddus, jellies- deli deli delicious
Almonds, cashews, pistachios crunch,
Every bite a delight each flavour so luscious.

Diwali oh Diwali
Making people together, hearts so bright,
Family and friends gather in joy tonight,
Sharing moments, laughter and cheer,
In the festival of lights we hold so dear.

Diwali oh Diwali

Making people buy chromatic colors,
Reds, yellows, blues- so lusty lusty lustrous,
Emeralds, rubies, sapphires so fine,
Glistening like stars shiny shiny shine.

Diwali oh Diwali
Making people welcome the goddess of wealth,
Good idols bring grace and stealth,
Inviting fortune, blessing divine,
As lamps are lit they sparkle and shine.

15. Endless Friendship

The bond that never bends,
Through all that time extends.
We walk side by side,
With hearts open wide,
For friendship never ends.

16. The Last Warning

Massive pollution fills the air,
Whispers heat in Earth's despair.
Each continent becomes so hot-
That's what our teacher taught.

Forests burn, rivers dry,
Nature's warning, we can't deny.
Glaciers melt, landslides slide,
Penguins lose their icy ride.

The trees cry and cry,
Yet humans pass by,
Birds fly in circles, lost in sky;
The future will be dark, no one asks why.

Oceans rise, and forests fall,
Natural disasters rise with it all.
We ignore the signs we see,
The next generation will never be free.

17. A Prehistoric Jurassic Journey

Hunter & scavenger,
Mighty Giganotosaurus, largest flesh eater.
Standing tall, measuring six meters,
Bird-like Troodon, brainiest of all.
At night, answering the call.
T-rex's sharp teeth, long and strong,
Curved like a tongs, they tear meat along.
Velociraptors, so small & agile,
A hunter so swift, so deadly and wild.

Horned & Armored,
Famous plated dinosaur—Stegosaurus,
A great evolution of earlier Scelidosaurus.
Euoplocephalus, with a long clubbed tail,
Still shorter than the big blue whale.
Seeing a rhino charge would be a scary sight,
But a three-plated Triceratops would bring a terrible fright.
Gastonia, belly low to the ground,

As it turned slowly, cautious all around.

Speedy dinosaur,
Hypsilophodon, furious & fast,
In a land so vast.
Compsognathus, turkey-sized,
A hunter small, yet full of pride.
Gallimimus, quick and spry,
Chasing prey as the days go by.
T-rex, so fast & big,
Feasting on meat, not keen on figs.

Gentle plant eater,
Diplodocus, with a giant bed,
Despite its small head.
Brachiosaurus, as heavy as seven elephants,
Reaching for treetops with ease and elegance.
Protoceratops, with horned beak,
Slicing through tough leaves to eat.
Plateosaurus, with small teeth, strong hand,
Grabbing leaves and bringing them to land.

18. The Legacy of Pride Land

Mufasa, king of Pride Rock's great land,
A lion noble, with strength to stand.
With a brother named Scar, whose heart was cold,
Mufasa's legacy, a tale of old.

Scar's destiny, dark and cruel,
Claiming life's not fair, a twisted rule.
Hyenas stamped, Mufasa in trouble,
Wild beasts gathered, ready to rumble.

Mufasa found as a stray,
Strength in him, though humble his way.
Mufasa, a brother, noble and true,
Pride Rock's sun rays kissed skies of blue.

Chikaguru's eyesight, so sharp and clear,
Predicts so well, making enemies fear.
Eshe teaches hunters, the antelope, the deer,
Guiding their path, as their prey draws near.

Rafiki, the Sage, the wise old baboon,
Spinning tales in the light of the moon.
From the smallest ant to the mighty antelope,
He taught respect, the thread of hope.

19. Tasmania- Nature's Symphony

Go take out a look, nature awaits,
No need to book, just open the gate.
Each sunrise paints the sky in gold,
Reminding that the sky is not old.

Delicate butterflies dance through the air,
Creating a world beyond compare.
Graceful waterfalls, like liquid poetry,
Whispers of peace, leaving serenity.

Tasmania's shore, where wild waves roar,
Inviting the wild from nature's door.
Tasmanian devils, fierce and bold,
Untamed, they roam wild and untold.

Wildflowers paint the earth with flair,
A vibrant carpet woven with care.
Trees whisper softly through rusting leaves,
Sharing ancient wisdom the earth believes.

20. The Language of Stones

"Look around, rocks are under your feet,
Black, tan, or brown, they lie so neat.
Green, blue, or even pink,
Sparkling with colors, more than you think."

Limestone is strong, the pyramids still stand today,
Diamonds are hardest, shining in every way.
Talc is the softest, gentle to the touch,
Some pumice rocks float, defying so much.
The moon is made of igneous stone,
A geode is dull, but inside it's unknown.
Obsidian, smooth as glass, dark and sleek,
A hidden beauty in rocks, waiting to speak.

Earth is like a giant rock factory,
Carrying secrets from ancient time,
From deep below to mountain peaks,
Rocks tell stories that never die.

21. The Light Between Worlds

Streaks of light, they fall to earth,
Weigh more than 9 buses, full of worth.
Most meteorites are from asteroids,
Fragments of space that time avoids.
Space rock rubs against the gas,
Creating heat as it burns fast.
Down to earth, they leave their trace,
A shooting star in time and space.
A flash of wonder, gone too soon,
A cosmic dance beneath the moon.

www.ingramcontent.com/pod-product-compliance
Lightning Source LLC
La Vergne TN
LVHW010947200726
843509LV00013B/2311